I0441217

Breeder's Digest

The Demographics of Decline

Dust Cover

What percentage of Money Transfers at a ghetto supermarket go to Federal prison inmates?

Why didn't Taino Indians want to go to heaven and opted to be burned at the inquisitor's stake instead?

How many calories of petroleum does it take to produce 1 calorie of food?

What is the cannibal record for human livers eaten by one man in a lifetime?

Why was Genghis Khan a humanitarian?

Where will you find the 15 million psychopaths in the United States?

Have you ever felt like a guinea pig in some unseen mastermind's laboratory, and would like evidence that your creeping sense of hierarchal insemination is justified?

If you are hungry for off-the wall factoids that point to where we came from and where we are headed, then the **Breeder's Digest** will give you all the ammunition you need to wage an unconventional dinner party discussion. Also includes the first five secrets of the universe according to Tarl Cabot, the 'Box Prophet', who sketched the secrets of human salvation on the inside of his cardboard home, with a 'spork' in his own blood, only to have some 'ecofreaks' shove his home, and the chance for mankind's salvation, into a compactor!

For Larry, survivor of 40 years under the gun—
keep ducking dude.

Contents

Breeder's Digest

© 2013 James LaFond

For the discerning breeder who plans on propagating, your friendly ghetto researcher offers this guide to some of the lesser known facts that may impact your personal reproductive policies, or at least assist you in educating your inheritors concerning little known things. Unless a source is cited to the right in brackets, the information below is derived from the author's own diligent research.

Initial Entry

Best evidence that the White House was once occupied by a human comes from my favorite quote by John Fitzgerald Kennedy concerning then President's Eisenhower's home: "The Tomb of The Well Known Soldier."

The United States has 5% of world population. [History Channel 2]

The United States has 25% of world prison population. [HC2]

Percentage of U.S citizens classified as black: 10% [HC2]

Percentage of the U.S. prison population classified as black: 40% [HC2]

One Baltimore area deli uses cold running water to cool down boiled potatoes, so that these potatoes may be mixed with the mayonnaise-based sauce without spoiling it. In order to properly cool them in this fashion takes 3 hours [according to the cook]. So that one 40 pound batch of potatoes may be so cooled, it requires 540 gallons of potable water, at the double faucet rate of 3 gallons per minute. Perhaps the World Bank would like to finance a potato salad factory in the Sudan?

In Maryland 'food stamp' benefits are distributed between the 6th and the 18th of each month.

Avoid discount food shopping on these days, unless you want to make a deal...

Heroin addicts will permit you to spend $20 dollars of their food stamp allotment for $10.

Crack-heads will permit you to spend $30 dollars of their sister's food stamp allotment for $10.

Percentage of Western Union money transfers sent from a Baltimore City food market to the FBOP [Federal Bureau of Prisons]: 30%

Grilling Season Edition

"...Abraham built an altar there, and laid the wood in order, and bound Isaac his son, and laid him on the altar, upon the wood..." [Genesis 22:9-13]

"...Burned shall he be at the fiery flame,

And his wife laden with fire wood..." [The Koran, Sura CXI]

The reason stated [circa 1600 A. D.] by one Cuban Taino Indian for burning at the stake rather than accepting Christ and going to heaven: "...because he would find more Christians there."

Daily Neanderthal dietary 'live-weight' [before you cook it] meat requirement circa 70,000 B.C.: 4 pounds per person, or 16 quarter-pounders—hold everything.

The number of petroleum calories it takes to produce 1 calorie of human food through modern cultivation methods: 10 [Zeitgeist, Rupert]

The maximum number of hearts one team of Aztec priests could rip out of living human breasts in one 12 hour work day: 720.

The number of indigenous Mexicans killed by Spanish conquistadors and their diseases between 1513 and 1605: 23,025,000 out of a total of 25,000,000.

And you wonder why Mexicans are so good at cutting grass…

According to Dante Justine, Harford County Maryland landscaping contractor, the 'man-value' of landscapers by race, is as follows:

"Mexicans are equal to half a man."

"White-boys are only one third of a man, and can't fight worth shit, so are at least easy to fire."

"Black guys are only one third of a man, and some can fight—and even those who can't think they can—so firing them is a pain in the ass. So why in hell would I hire them?"

"Asian landscapers? You're kidding right?"

The number of Crow Indian livers eaten by 19th Century Mountain Man Liver-eating Johnson: 247! If you were a Sioux throwing a pot-luck party who else would you invite to your 'bring-your-own-enemy-organ' cookout but good old Liver-eatin'? [Tannahill, Flesh and Blood, page 142]

Eight Uplifting Facts

Quote of the Week

When advising a pair of young fighters about networking with martial arts instructors, Arturo Gabriel, Puerto Rican martial arts instructor, said the following:

"Flips [Filipinos] are tricky to deal with. They will always demand some kind of consideration before they give you anything... They're easier to deal with than the Chinese. The Chinese won't give you a thing until you marry into the family or swear allegiance. Now Koreans, you just throw money at them."

California State prison population: 119,542

Percentage of California State prison beds currently occupied: 149.5

-LA Times

Percentage of California State prisoners who are mentally ill: 30%

-NY Times

The number of hours it takes the average boxer to learn how to hit the speed bag: 6

The number of earthlings who think the above fact is worthy of consideration: 1

Frequency a Baltimore City bus patron will be panhandled at an uncovered bus stop: 1 in 14

Frequency a Baltimore City bus patron will be panhandled at a covered bus stop: 1 in 3

Frequency a Baltimore City bus patron will be approached by missionaries at a major transfer point: 1 in 7

Empire Earth

Notable Quote

"This idea that what you love is often the opposite of what you want to be is a central paradox of masculinity."

-Jack Donovan 7/29/13

The Empire Strikes Back

Death Star Online!

DARPA, the hideous acronym for the U.S. military's premier doom science department, is well on it's way to developing a submersible drone mother ship, an underwater aircraft carrier for the insect-size to model plane-size exploding gadgets that shall soon enable video game players to rule the world.

Number of nations in which the U.S. maintains military bases: 153

U.S. military bases worldwide: 900

U.S. bases on the island of Okinawa: 38 [Where do the locals live?]

U.S. troops in Okinawa commit how many more violent crimes than U.S. service personnel worldwide? The sad answer is four times normal.

The number of rapes and murders committed against Japanese citizens living on Okinawa by U.S service men stationed there, per month: 2

The number of U.S Marines required to rape a 12-year-old Japanese girl and still fulfill their social drinking commitments: 3

-source, Blowback by Chalmers Johnson, and Rt.com

The Body Count

The number of Iraqi civilians killed during the course of U.S. operations from 2004 thru 2012: 1 million

The number of 'depicted' deaths seen by an American child before adulthood: 8,000

-source, Culture In Decline.com

The number of slaves owned by the first president of the U.S.: 300

-source, Jacque Fresco

Welcome to The Homeland Jose and Jacques

© 2013 James LaFond

"It's only seven a.m. and I've already seen a drug deal...at the McDonald's drive-through."

-home improvement contractor, 8/1/13

On 7/31/13 Senator Dianne Feinstein, speaking at a Senate Judiciary Committee Hearing, said that thirteen terrorist 'events' [a category that is less than a plot] have been disrupted [presumably meaning kidnapping and torturing some Pakistani bakery owner] "in The Homeland". As she spoke, behind the Senate 'Intelligence' Bimbo, a nominally human drone held up a map, indicating that North America is one nation.

'Anti-terror squads' [body-armored goons] conduct about one hundred home searches per week in New York State, largely based on tips provided by employers, neighbors, and internet sources [such as backpack inquires].

The number of U.S. government employees and mercenaries who have access to classified information [including your phone and email metadata]: 4.8 million

Tons of radioactive water leaked into the Pacific by the Fukushima reactor daily: 300

Radioactive water yet to be released into the Pacific: 20,000 tons

-Source, RT.com

Non-border states in which Mexican drug cartels conduct major operations [with machine guns supplied by the CIA, I might add]: 9 interior U.S. states

-Source, Associated Press

The number of criminal gangs with operatives currently operating within the U.S. Armed Services [largely to acquire military training and equipment]: 53

-Source, FBI National Gang Intelligence Center

The amount of time that, according to genius social engineer Jacque Fresco, it requires for the modern media to achieve total mind control of a large enough portion of the population of Planet Earth to result in tacit universal compliance: 3 months

-source, a Venus Project interview

Are You Breeding Competitively?

© 2013 James LaFond

"This is WIC [Women Infants Children] not BIC [Bimbos Idiots Crazies] lady!"

-Grocery manager explaining to a customer why she must purchase the store brand peanut butter with her Department of Agriculture food voucher and not the jar with the cartoon on it

Breeding rates by race circa 1920:

1. whites 3.0

2. yellows 4.5

3. browns 4.5

4. blacks 6.0

-source, Lothrop Stoddard, The Rising Tide of Color

Current British Breeding rates:

1. Anglo 1.5

2. Islamic 3.5

Stoddard warned you non-breeding Brits about being out-screwed 100 years ago. By 2040 you will be hard-pressed to find a pub in Londonabad.

The history subject that has been dropped from French public schools in an attempt to cater to French Islamic sensibilities: World War Two!

Unable to safely reference the Holocaust to Islamic students, French educators decided that continuing to acknowledge that WWII occurred, would be hypocritical.

-source, Hoover Institute online broadcast

The punishment meted out to a Saudi blogger for 'insulting Islam': 600 lashes and 7 years in prison

-rt.com

The cost in dollars to each U.S. household of the Second Iraq War: $50,000

-source, Free Domain Radio

Breeder's Digest

Celebrities who renounced their U.S. citizenship in the first quarter of 2013: Tina Turner [getting laid in Switzerland] and Bobby Fischer [being smart elsewhere]

-rt.com

Same-race online dating preferences by U.S. whites who have stated on their profile that race did not matter: white men 90%; white women 97%

-source, Freakonomics by Levitt and Dubner

Postmodern Slavery, and the Priest-King of Gotham

© 2013 James LaFond

"You're gonna have face-recognition software. People are working on that. We're gonna have more visibility and less privacy…It's scary, but what's the difference whether the drone is up in the air or on the buildings."

-3/23/13, NYC Mayor Bloomberg

Bloomberg's oligarchical standing: 27 billion dollars; 7th richest oligarch in the U.S.A.

Bloomberg's 5/20/13 career recommendation for aspiring university students: be a plumber

Since 5% of Gotham peasants live in public housing, and 20% of crime is committed by these same people, Bloomberg has suggested finger printing all public housing residents, igniting a storm of liberal scorn.

What is the sense in complaining about the fingerprinting, when, as Bloomberg pointed out on 4/26/13, "You're never going to know where our cameras are."

4.4 million New Yorkers have been stopped and frisked under Mayor Bloomberg's controversial profiling initiative. 6% of these stops resulted in charges being filed against the suspect.

"Packing More Guns Than the Air Force"

The oppressed genius who rapped the above line was arrested and charged along with 19 others for running guns from South Carolina to Gotham. 250 guns were confiscated, and he was said to travel with up to 14 on his person. The ring largely relied on discount 'Chinatown buses' for transportation.

-source, rt.com

Rate of increase in diagnosed psychopathy from 1998 thru 2013: double

-source, Free Domain Radio

Worldwide value of people sold into slavery in 2012: 42 billion dollars

Common occupations of slaves: sex object; domestic servant; panhandler

Notable countries of origin for slaves: Russia and other former Soviet republics; Eastern Europe; Black Africa; China; the Philippines

Slaves are known to be shipped to and owned in non-black Islamic Nations, Israel, and the United States of America.

-source, rt.com

Nuking 'The Middle Eastern'

© 2013 James LaFond

Quote of the Week:

"The ossified tadpole hole you were born into."

-Stefan Molyneux

Runner up:

"I was at a bar last week with two Towson State students, females. You would think there would be some intelligence there. But the one begins speaking about Syria, saying, "We should have one big nuclear bomb to drop on the Middle Eastern. [Like it's an airline or something]These people are terrible. All of the Syrian's should just be killed.'"

"Then her friend—mind you a friend of a few years, not someone who she just met—says, 'But I'm Syrian.'"

"So the first one responds, 'I thought you were from New Jersey. Well, there are good people in any group. But I'm sure the good Syrians are all over here now. So we should just bomb what's left.'"

"What do you say to that? How do your reason with people like that?"

-Oliver

You don't reason with them Oliver. You point them at the T.V. again so that they can soak up the Two Minutes of Hate at 6:00 p.m. It is oh so important that they know who the enemy is. We would not want her nuking New Jersey for instance...

Current world resources held by the richest 1%: 70%

-Culture In Decline, Episode #6

Pay increases since 1978 for CEOs: 870%

Overall income increase since 1978: 15%

People who are emerging out of poverty in India and China per month: 50,000

Child abuse by women is how much more common than that by men: X3

-Free Domain Radio

People living in cities in 1800: 3%

People living in cities in 2008: 50%

People living in cities projected for 2050: 70%

Human rat race capital: Mexico City with 18 million people and 6 million cars

-Awake, March 2012

Global unemployment in 2010, according to the IMF: 210 million

According to a 2012 report by the Mental Health Foundation of London:

65% of office workers experience 'office rage'

33% of Britons are not on speaking terms with their neighbors

32% of Britons claim to have a close friend or family member who has trouble controlling anger

The conclusion of the week is to not marry that New Jersey girl who migrated from Syria via London. She's already pissed off one third of the time. Imagine what a bitch she'll be after we 'nuke the Middle Eastern'.

'People Wish To Be Bobble Heads'

© 2013 James LaFond

-actor, Ed Asner

Quote of the Week

"I'm drinking absinthe mixed with the blood of statists."

-Stefan Molyneux

Population Expansion Trivia

Most prolific father: Ismael Ibn Sharife with 900 children

Most prolific mother: Feodora Vassilyev with 16 sets of twins, 7 sets of triplets, and 4 sets of quadruplets.

-VSauce

Population Reduction Trivia

In July 1,035 terrorists, including 140 high-ranking Al Qaeda leaders, escaped from the Abu Ghraib and Taji prisons in Iraq [conveniently close to Syria].

-Sunday Times of London

Malpractice insurance increase per surgeon in 2011: 250,000 dollars per year

-Interview by author of anonymous doctor

Number of Americans who doubt the findings of the 911 Commission: 38%

Number of architects and engineers who doubt the findings of the 911 Commission concerning the structural failure of the Twin Towers: 2,000

Number of authors critical of the 911 Commission who have mysteriously killed themselves at crime scenes later secured by the FBI: 1 and counting

-RT.com

Wage Slave Trivia

Federal Minimum wage: $7.25 per hour

California minimum wage: $8.00

Washington State minimum wage: $9.19 per hour

-RT.com

The wages of a union supermarket clerk in Maryland in 1992: $11.40 per an hour

The wages for a union supermarket clerk in Maryland in 2013: $10.80 per an hour

-the author

Who's Killing Who and How?

© 2013 James LaFond

Quote of The Week

"They only come when tradition is threatened."

-a Mennonite rape victim on her colony's theocratic enforcers

Number of Syrian rebels currently fighting: 100,000

Number of rebel factions: 1,000

Number of rebels who are Islamist jihadists: 50,000

Rebels are currently being supplied by: U.S., France, Britain, and other, apparently pro Islamist, patrons.

-RT.com

Of U.S. jobs created in 2013 how many were fulltime: 3%

-Trends Journal

Homicides in U.S. committed with a firearm: 69.3%

Five most lethal municipalities in 2012:

1. New York City: 515 murders

2. Chicago: 431 murders

3. Detroit: 386 murders

4. Philadelphia: 331 murders

5. Los Angeles: 299

-FBI

Adjusted for population the list looks like this:

1. Detroit

2. Philadelphia

3. Chicago

4. New York

5. Los Angeles

Baltimore, with its relatively small population, would place between Detroit and Philly, with nearly as many murders as LA, which has many times the population.

The record for most people shot in one back alley dice game is held by Baltimore at 7 hit, 1 fatality

-the author

Your Offseason Vacation Guide

© 2013 James LaFond

Quote of the Week

"The devil claims the tenth scholar as his own…"

-Bram Stoker, Dracula

U.S. citizens who disappear every year: 2,000

Missing U.S. children: 50,000

-FBI

Unaccounted for [runaways that nobody cares about] children: 100,000

-some bleeding heart pack of liberal whiners

The number of years it requires U.S. military personnel to torture a 15-year-old POW to confess to five war crimes based on his alleged killing of a U.S. service man with a grenade: 8! Really guys? I think we need some Turkish prison guards down there in Gonads-for-Police-Dogs Bay.

The number of shoulder fired weapons required to defend a cigarette shop in Tripoli Libya: 6 [one fully automatic]

The mayor of Benghazi Libya: Huda 'The Executioner'

Most popular Libyan pickup truck accessory: automatic antiaircraft cannon

Facilities used for political prisons in the new American-liberated Libya: elementary schools and zoos. I really must object on behalf of the original inmates, who have been displaced where?

Gun stalls on Al Rhasid Street in Tripoli are manned by boys whose inventory include: batons, tazers, hand guns, pump shotguns and M-16s. It beats school!

-VICE

I have no current price on a weekend getaway for two at the Tripoli Motel Six.

Beggars at The Gate

"America is finally starting to behave like other countries."

-Ajay on the 10/5/13 D.C. immolation

In medieval times the lords and ladies who ruled Christendom under the wise stewardship of the largest child-abuse union in human history believed in charity; specifically that giving to the needy would get them to heaven. On Alms Day the castle gate would open, and The Lady would emerge to bestow her change upon the most wretched examples of her husband's earthbound slaves, while he was out patrolling the countryside for the least wretched examples of his slave farmers' daughters. In order for this scheme to enjoy the stability of perpetuity, it would not due to fix any of the causes for poverty, for without the impoverished there could be no meaningful charity, and without meaningful charity, how was The Lady of the castle supposed to earn a place in heaven for her and her less pious husband?

Is it any different today?

Yesterday I was breakfasting at a diner, which had the overhead TV tuned into one of the Imperial Television News Networks. Two rich women, and one rich man, were charged with comforting me. They spoke to a guest, a criminal named Nancy with a Greek-sounding last name, who is part of the corporate junta that owns me. The conversation was concerned with the possible interruption of poverty benefits due to a disagreement between the two factions of the junta. While I was supposed to believe I was viewing journalism, I could arrive at no conclusion that did not place these four rich people firmly in the same interest group. Nancy was 'The Lady at the gate', promising alms for the loyal in good time.

Some Related Facts Concerning Average Annual Income of U.S. Citizens

Senior on Social Security: $12,000

Soldier on Deployment in Afghanistan: $38,000

The Salaries of the Corporate Junta, Enjoyed for Life!

President: $450,000

Congressman/woman: $174,000

Speaker of the House: $223,500

Senate Majority/Minority Leader: $194,400

Why Karachi Pakistan Has the Most Honest Politicians on Earth

© 2013 James LaFond

The three underdeveloped nations that have not ratified the United Nations Human Rights Treaty—which among other unreasonable provisions bars the execution of children: South Sudan; Somalia; and Detroit—I mean the Unites States of America.

The nation with the least creative naming tradition is Vietnam, where 40% of the population have the last name of Nguyen.

-VSauce

The most powerful woman in the world was the Mongol Empress Duragene, who was regent of the largest land empire ever from 1242 to 1246.

-Hardcore History

The number of people who win the lottery for new vehicle registrations in Beijing China is 1 in 53.

In 2001 In Italy the sale of bicycles exceeded the sale of cars.

74% of 599 Japanese alleged child rapists admitted that their primary reason for using social networking sites was to have sex with minors.

-Awake, October 2013

In Karachi Pakistan, population 18,000,000 plus, there are believed to be 600 active 'target killers', who earn between $550 and $1100 per murder. 80% of these hits are ordered by politicians and 20% by criminals.

-Vice

Where Are America's 15 Million Psychopaths?

© 2013 James LaFond

The following two lists are adapted from the book The Wisdom of Psychopaths by Kevin Dutton.

The Ten Professions Most Favored by Psychopaths

1. CEO

2. Lawyer

3. Media

4. Sales

5. Surgeon

6. Journalist

7. Cop

8. Clergy

9. Chef [What are these guys doing, molesting their interns?]

10. Civil Servant [an oxymoronic parasite if ever there was one]

The top eight professions afford the psycho with a large amount of creative control over others. Keep in mind that virtually all politicians are lawyers. Remember that in pre-modern times, military establishments were run by the same type of people who head corporations today. Today's general is more like a football coach who agrees to kiss copious amounts of ass than any of the famous generals of yesteryear.

The Ten Professions Least Practiced by Psychopaths

1. Care aid [Yes, changing bed pans is a drag compared to snuffing teenage hitchhikers.]

2. Nurse

3. Therapist

4. Crafts

5. Beautician [I can well image these are often the abused grooming slaves of media icons.]

6. Charity worker

7. Teacher

8. Artist

9. Doctor [who, presumably declines to cut people up]

10. Accountant

I would make one observation about this list, that these people are often employed in a subservient capacity to the psycho professions.

The Care & Feeding of Barbarian Whelps and Civilized Brats-to-be

© 2013 James LaFond

"I've got to grow old in a world populated by these people."

-Stefan Molyneux

The above child advocate and philosopher provided most of the information below. I bet you can't tell which items I inserted from my own research.

Children who have been spanked have a 3-5 point lower IQ score than those who have been raised by permissive hippie types.

Genghis Khan was a little-appreciated child advocate, permitting conquered people shorter than a wagon wheel to live. If you were a Turk in 1228, you better have been a child.

A 2013 Brown University study indicated that breastfeeding improves brain development.

Mongol children learned to ride before they could walk. You gear heads might want to try a modern version of this vocational toddler training.

Parents who participate in the federal WIC program are less likely to breast feed.

In the 1970s Nestle planted phony uniformed nurses in South African hospitals to promote formula use. This initiative was a success. Due to the hazardous nature of the local drinking water available to mix with the formula many children sickened and died as a result.

Apache boys were made to run long distances in arid mountains with their mouths full of water without swallowing it. They did not drink Similac!

Frequency of breastfeeding by major U. S. racial group:

Asian = 86%

Hispanic = 81%

White = 78%

Black = 68%

I have placed this study here in the Breeder's Digest largely as an attempt to seize the moral high ground, and win, once and for all, an ongoing debate with a lesbian tennis fan. When she declared Venus Williams to be far more desirable a mate than her sister Serena, I objected, pointing out that Serena would be better equipped to bear and nurse the small army of combat athletes I had in mind. Now Ajay, the information above proves that I'm more than a sexist breeder, but one that cares, cares for the children and their fledgling minds—a veritable pillar of altruism!

Exploit This

© 2013 James LaFond

Natural resources exported from Africa and Latin America compared to aid imported: 19-1

Global wealth controlled by richest 1% in 1970s: 10%

Global wealth controlled by richest 1% in 2000s: 20-70% (Well, it's better than giving it to the crack-heads.)

-Bleeding heart liberal Chrystal Freeland

Unemployment in Mogadishu Somalia: 70%

3 out of every 5 impoverished people on earth are under 18.

-A Somalia graduate student on TedTalks

Percentage of the average English speaker's vocabulary usage that consists of swear-words: 0.7

The state whose citizens swear the most during recorded customer service calls: Ohio

The state you want your calls coming from if you are a customer service operator: Washington (My pothead friend says it is because pot is basically legal in Washington.)

The most used swear-word is F***

The runner up swear-word is S***

-Vsauce

California's state prison system is currently at 150% of capacity.

The 113th Congress has passed fewer bills than any other modern congress, with only 56 bills being enacted into law, including one on the dimensions of Major League Baseball Hall-of-Fame collectable coins. (RT reporters did spot congressional aids hauling in 12-packs of beer.)

The U.S. War on Yemeni marriages has just scored another victory, with a drone strike against another wedding in Yemen, which has produced 15 bodies.

The online fact checking service PolitiFact has just given the award for Lie of the Year to some abused child from Chicago, for his statement that, "If you like your health care plan, you can keep it."

-RT.com

Chickenshit Apocalypse Trivia

© 2014 James LaFond

Percentage of chicken breast meat sold in U.S. supermarkets that is infected with bacteria: 97%

-The Ghetto Grocer

Of a survey of periodicals in a relative's periodical collection, the dominant advertised product by decade was:

1910s = household goods

1950s = cigarettes

1970s = cars

2010s = smart phones

-Author

Unemployment rate among Europeans 20-24 years of age: 63%

-The Guardian

Some required Zombie Apocalypse supplies, according to James Wesley, Rawles, author of How To Survive the End of The World as we Know It:

Battle rifle ammunition = 2-6,000 rounds

Primary handgun ammunition = 800 to 2,400 rounds

Riot gun = 500 to 1,500 rounds

Rice per an adult per year = 30 pounds dry weight

Three items you probably wouldn't think of but definitely want on hand:

1. Food grade PVC buckets [The Ghetto Grocer says, "Get them from your neighborhood supermarket for free. Send a cute chick and have her wink at the manager when she asks—a stack of buckets will materialize as if by magic."]

2. Aluminum foil—the duct tape you don't know about

3. Clorox bleach—and you dope fiends trying to pass your piss test by drinking bleached water thought you were crazy!

4. And, although he did not make this reference, based on his work, I think your chances of survival will go from 1% to 50% if you own your own squad of special operations soldiers, an armored fighting vehicle, and a really big siphon hose—and an out-of-work hooker from East Baltimore to operate that indispensable piece of equipment.

Over Where?

© 2014 James LaFond

"You are what they say you are."

-Jack Donavan, NPI speech from 2013

U.S. homeless rate: 7%

U.S. veteran homeless rate: 13%

Unemployment rate for veterans under 25: 25%

U.S. health care cost increase since 2000: 200%

Annual income for U. S. Army private of 2 years: $40,400

Annual income for U.S. Army captain, 6 years: $93,000

Military commissary food discount: 30% [that means it is being sold at the wholesale cost]

Pentagon retirement budget: 4.5 billion

Veterans who have earned a Pentagon pension: 17%

-Yahoo news

To date U.S. taxpayers have paid $150 million to 43 Afghan companies who are known [according to the SIGAR] to finance attacks on U.S. soldiers.

Current U.S. troop strength in Afghanistan is 37,500 [not counting approximately 95,000 mercenaries]

The Pentagon projects the need for 10,000 troops to remain in country just to protect American officials expected to be left behind after 2014.

The death rate for Afghan security forces increased by 80% from 2012 to 2013

The Afghan Army's annual attrition rate is 34%, having lost 67,000 troops through death and desertion in 2013.

Currently 100 Afghan troops are dying per week.

-RT.com

According to the DOJ 49% of prison rapes are committed by correctional officers.

According to the DOJ of all prison rapes reported, only 45% are referred for prosecution.

According to the DOJ only 1% of those corrections officers charged with prison rape are convicted.

-RT.com

Okay class, for this week's project write a 500 to 1,000 word paper describing whether you would rather serve in the Afghan Army or spend time in an American corrections facility—and why. Have the paper on my desk by Friday morning or report to the janitor [the big scary looking dude on work release] for bubblegum removal detail.

Getting Ahead in Saudi Arabia

© 2014 James LaFond

African nations where U.S. military operations were conducted in 2012-2013: 49

U.S. Military operations in Africa, 2011-2013: 1,000

U.S. special operations troops operating in Uganda in March 2014: 150

Nuke commanders fired by USAF in 2014: 9

Unmanned space plane record: 469 days in orbit and counting

-rt.com

Worldwide deaths attributed to air pollution in 2012: 7 million

-World Health Organization

Baltimore City police officers arrested for vice crimes in neighboring municipalities in the first quarter of 2014: 1 per month

-WBAL TV.com

Beheadings in Saudi Arabia [done with a nice crusader-style sword I might add]

2010: 27, with 5 being foreigners

2011: 82, with 28 being foreigners—ouch!

2012: 79, with 27 being foreigners

2013: 78, not certain about the number of foreigners

2014: 12 impious heads and counting!

-Associated Press

Reality TV Idea

7 Baltimore City cops hire out to the Saudis as construction site security; beating the shit out of migrant construction workers from India and Malaysia, etc. The viewers who correctly guess how

many of these cops are sentenced to death at the swordsman's hand for the various vice crimes they are bound to commit in the course of their employment, will be eligible for a million dollar drawing.

Homeland Insecurity and Urine Terrorism

© 2014 James LaFond

The Department of Homeland Security deports 400,000 'border crossers' per year, accounting for 70% of total deportations.

Judicial deportations in the U.S. have been on the decline since 2009.

Total immigration enforcement is at the highest levels in U.S. history.

Nationwide record store sales are declining at 10-15% per year.

86% of Nevada land is owned by the federal government.

80% of wild horses in the U.S. reside in Nevada, where they enjoy government benefits. I wonder if they live in trailer parks.

On 4/16/14 in Portland Oregon a teenager urinated in the Mt. Tabor Reservoir, resulting in the 'flushing' of 38-million gallons of water. Did this guy have a radioactive bladder, or what? A couple hundred of these urine terrorists could dehydrate the nation if a half pint of piss can poison 38 million gallons of water!

General Mills does offer internet coupons, but if you print them out and use them you have agreed to forced arbitration and give up your right to a jury trial, should you find yourself in litigation with them. Read that fine print.

2014's Worst Jobs in America

1. Lumberjack, 24k

2. Print journalist, 37k

3. Enlisted military personnel, 29k

4. Taxi driver, 23k

-Source, Aljazeera America

Breeding, Feeding and Culling in Harm City U.S.A.

© 2014 James LaFond

"Isn't it astonishing that people like you and I, who have never been on welfare, order our entire life around food stamp distributions? I've never spent a food stamp, or had an EBT cash card. But I can't go on vacation between the sixth and the sixteenth. And if food stamps and EBT cash were cut tomorrow, our hours—our income—would get cut the day after tomorrow. You know we're hostage slaves. We serve the welfare queens, and, if these payments ever stop, we won't make it off the lot."

-Baltimore City supermarket department manager

Benefits For Being A Single Unwed Mother in Baltimore

Rent is fixed at about $100 per month, or about 10% of actual cost, with the landlord receiving the balance of the rent from a government agency.

Variable energy assistance

$30 to $90 worth of WIC vouchers per child five years or less, per month

$200 EBT cash per child under 18, per month

$200 'food stamp' credit per child under 18, per month

The cap on child-based benefits is five. So be careful not to hatch egg number six until welfare vector number one has reached age 18. If this is not practical, then make sure your daughters get knocked up by age 14, so that they will begin drawing benefits for their hatchlings. Daughters are therefore preferable, so let the boys play in the street as toddlers and join gangs before puberty to make way for more daughters.

In city markets where black drug gangs predominate in the underworld, cash purchases reach record highs at the end of the month as the army of baby's mammas demand snack food and soft drink money from their nomadic mates. This is a reciprocal relationship, for when 'stamps' come out, she will spend much of her allotment on steak, shrimp, and other delicacies for herself and her baby's daddy, while feeding the children ramen noodles and chicken dogs.

The most expensive items purchased with food stamps are from least to most dear:

1. Uncooked thawed shrimp for about $30 for the typical 2-pound order. These cannot be bought steamed, though they may be bought chilled from a retail case. The legal stipulation is that they must not be 'hot'.

2. Snow crab clusters, with the typical order ranging from $30-$70. This is one of the most expensive items per pound that can be purchased in a food store outside of the spice section. Speaking of the spice section, you know when drug gangs are wholesaling out of your neighborhood when the garlic powder sales increase geometrically, as they use the powder to foil the noses of drug-sniffing police dogs.

3. The most expensive food stamp item that is commonly purchased—usually one to a food stamp customer per month—is decorated cakes. These range in price from $40 to $200 dollars, and feature such crucial nutritive ingredients as photos printed

in icing. The best cake decorators in any chain are sent to low income locations.

Narcostate News Beat

Baltimore city police have 690 tazers. After officers killed a patient with tazers in a city hospital [he was not a suspect], the Baltimore PD has announced that their officers will soon be certified to use these tazers.

Fixed position [corner] drug dealing is now conducted primarily through gas stations and other retail outlets. Gas stations specialize in retailing 'Spice' synthetic marijuana at $30-$60 per ounce. Much of Baltimore EBT cash distributions go toward purchasing spice, menthol cigarettes, and liquor at small retail outlets.

Not wanting to leave their customers defenseless, local retailers I have visited keep a selection of tactical fighting knives for sale on their counter at deep discounts. The prices ranged from $2 to $10 for tactical folders with blade lengths from 2 to 5 inches.

Much of the urban white Social Security payouts to disabled middle-aged people [most drug addicts end up disabled by middle age] are currently going to drug purchases, primarily of prescription narcotics purchased on city buses and at mass transit hubs, the deals made on free federal phones.

Most of the urban white welfare payout is enabling the drug economy: subsidized rent maintains crack houses and heroin dens; EBT cash is spent on liquor and cigarettes; food stamps are sold for 50 cents on the dollar to middle class families, police officers, and urban ministers. After the 16th these white welfare recipients resort to panhandling, theft and prostitution to make ends meet. The kids pretty much starve all week and then get shipped off to a grandmother or aunt to fatten up over the weekend while the parents are too intoxicated to offer even the most basic nurturing.

-from author interviews and observations

The American Meta-Crimescape

-12 U.S. cities account for nearly 25% of crime nationwide.

-Chicago has as many murders as Japan, and a murder rate similar to such civil war ravaged African nations as Rwanda, and Sierra Leone.

-New Orleans has a murder rate 10 times the national average. If it were a nation it would have the second highest murder rate in the world.

-Baltimore has a higher murder rate than South Africa, which is in the top ten most violent nations worldwide.

-Detroit has a higher murder rate than Columbia, and there is a war going on in Columbia!

-80% of U.S. crime is gang related

-83% of murder victims in Chicago have criminal records

-91% of murder victims in Baltimore have criminal records

-Free Domain Radio, Violence in America

'And Your Mongrel Children Too!'

A Race-mixing Road Trip

© 2014 James LaFond

In 2009 Ajay, thirty-something black woman, drove Charles and Adam [both in their early twenties], and me, down to Chesapeake Virginia to fight on an MMA card. On the way down Charles was ripping into Adam about the possibility of dating the girl that Adam had fallen for at our last event. This was made even worse when the instructor of the young lady called me and said, "I don't usually do this, but my female student really wanted me to get Charles' number for her!"

After the way Charles had already been picking on the junior member of the team, Ajay gave me a 'how could you' look when I relayed the message. Adam retreated into his gaming magazine and Charles seemed to ease off. Ajay breathed a sigh of relief and then Charles made an inclusive overture, "Do you play that game?"

Adam perked up, "Yeah, I really prefer their character development scheme."

Charles then—as a certain serpent must have in a garden a long time ago—slithered in for the silent kill, "Don't worry Adam, the female characters in your role playing game will not judge you and find you wanting."

Ajay asked me if she should pull over so they could fight, but Adam—ever a fan of a nicely timed blow—laughed the loudest.

I included that bit of cruel camaraderie just to set the stage, to let the reader know that we were a fairly thick-skinned bunch. And, if we declined to laugh at someone who is clearly insane out of respect for the damned, it must be very clear that they are just that—nuts!

We tumbled into some kind of burger joint in Virginia and ended up sitting in a booth across from an 80 year old woman, a small lady with curly white hair, light clothing, and a black purse, who glared at us with intense hatred.

This woman just kept staring at us with a fury that had me convinced that the ghost of the Fuhrer had finally spun off of an arm of the swastika and landed—in this old broad.

Her eyes were black pinpoints that I only met once. I once saw Ron Bone after he had taken eight hits of speed, smoked a half ounce of hash, drank a case of wine, ate to horse tranquilizers, and ate a whole ice cube tray of blue unicorn acid, and his eyes were not that reptilian.

She spoke a lot, some in mumbles, some clearly, and for minutes. We did not want to laugh at her, and all looked away. But she would keep saying things. I was so afraid that I was going to breakdown laughing in front of a crazy woman that I shut most of what she said out.

Ajay was looking ahead at her hands on the table. Adam was actually making eye contact with this crazy bitch. Charles was looking up at the ceiling and rubbing his mouth and jaw, trying to keep the muscles from tearing his face into a wicked smile.

She was homing in on Ajay and I. She had gotten the idea that Ajay and I were practicing miscegeny and had somehow produced these two white guys— well, Adam is Italian American, so we can blame him for the misunderstanding.

We nervously refused to meet her gaze when she demanded it. I looked at Charles across the table, barely maintaining his composure and holding his mouth shut with one hand. Then the lady said something nasty to Ajay and capped off the statement with, "And your mongrel children too!"

That was it.

I started to chuckle.

Charles was turning red.

Ajay was giggling like a seated hula dancer, and then I snorted—done, put a fork in us. We burst into uproarious laughter, with Adam sounding like a German shepherd that just realized it could laugh like a human. We piled out of there to the car. I don't even remember what I ate if anything.

Where was Adam?

He was in there speaking with the woman who had become the Oracle of Adolf Hitler.

I have never laughed so hard with others in all my life. Possibly the biggest objection I have to the liberal trend toward political correctness in America, is not fear of some Orwellian future, but fear of living in a world where I could not meet that insane witch at a burger joint, and have a laugh of a much higher quality than the caliber of whatever food might be had there.

Adam, Charles, Ajay, if you remember anything about this that I left out, please put it in the comments below. I laughed so hard it shorted out my memory.

«

Adam Swinder   June 17, 2014 11:13 PM EDT

A couple of things that I can add from my end:

It was April 2007, not 2009.

The burger joint was a Wendy's, if I recall correctly.

I don't remember anything leading up to the blow out where she started screaming at us, but I do remember talking to her as she got up and just started walking around, extricating the most virulent verbal diarrhea I'd ever heard with these ears.

And to think I'd almost forgotten about this incident, strange how being a full contact stickfighter recalibrates your Weird-Shit-o'-Meter.

Union Shaft

A Gurgle From the Bowels of Our Beneficent Machine

© 2014 James LaFond

I worked a union job for 15 years and still receive pension updates. I know a number of people who have planned their life around these unfunded private liabilities.

I recently received the 'Annual Funding Notice For United Food And Commercial Workers Unions And Participating Employers Pension Fund'

The total number of participants stands at 14,660. Of this number 7,358 were active [working and contributing to the pension], 2,557 were retired or separated from service and receiving benefits, and 4,745 were retired or separated and entitled to future benefits [that would be me].

The year 2010 saw the funded percentage dip below 80%

The year 2011 saw the funded percentage of the plan at 76.5%

The year 2012 saw the fund down to 66.3% funded

The year 2013 saw a slight rebound with 67.4% funded

I am no money guy. I have $9.11 in the bank. My opinion doesn't mean much here.

But, I have access to the backend of this website!

In light of the fact that the union workforce continues to shrink, when those 4,000+ people 'entitled to future benefits' come on line, and some of those 7,000+ 'active participants' move on to non union work, I think things are going to look a lot like seven sailors bailing and seven sailors piling in without buckets while some Manhattan sea worm continues to burrow into the hull of their retirement boat.

The notice does go on to point out that the fund has been in 'endangered status' ever since it dipped below 80%, and has been operating according to a federally sanctioned 'rehabilitation plan' since 2010.

The fund will fall under a higher level of scrutiny should the plan dip below 65% and earn 'critical status' evaluation.

I have never counted on this pension, or believed in my wildest dreams that it would survive long enough to pay me anything. However, most of the people that work for this union are, should we say, easily led. Probably the only thing the pension plan has going for it is the active participants are hard working, and that almost all of the participants smoke.

No one in government or the media will care much when this plan goes belly up. I am wondering about the many plans administered by our State and Federal masters. Baltimore area cops have a really hard time containing alcohol induced unrest by teens in June. How could they possibly deal with economic induced unrest by adults all year round?

'Rat-Smack City'

© 2014 James LaFond

The 'Can't Crack an Egg' Award of 2014 goes out to an example of one of the worst practitioners of ground-and-pound-while-bald-wannabe-MMA-California-cop-Fu in all of fistic history. An Officer of Cloven Hoof scored 10-15 rights hands on one crazy chick and could not even get her cuffed. The lady was walking on a freeway, which is against the law everywhere in the U.S. unless an alien invasion is in progress. So, she certainly deserved to be taken down and out.

But dude, you can't whoop one girl's ass? And it's not like it was Rhonda I'm-afraid-to-misspell-her-last-name was your opponent. Let the hair grow or go down to Hunting Beach and talk to Tito about putting some guns in your ground game. This happened on Freeway 10 near La Brea Avenue. Please be compassionate and leave a pink boxing glove there in commemoration of Officer Limp Fist's manhood.

On the upside, Chicago kill shots are improving over last summer, with their boyz racking up 11 kills in 60 shootings. Another year of improvement like this and we should be able to stage a championship shoot out between the Baltimore Boyz and the Chicago Boyz. Perhaps we could use Toledo Ohio as a battleground?

You tree huggers will be glad to hear that we have been in a 10 year cooling cycle, with U.S. temps down 0.7 degrees. I am personally hoping for another ice age so that my Neanderthal genome can once again count for something other than sunburn. But with all of those earth mother rapists burning fossil fuels there might be a postponement of my knuckle-dragging landbridge reunion.

Heroin futures are up in the Panty Waist State my friends. Maryland is officially the most heroin addicted state of the Union with 10% of Marylanders doing the dope fiend lean! There is no way this could have anything to do with our five star welfare benefits package.

The rat Mecca of the U.S. is New York.

Second in rat population is Boston.

Third is Baltimore, and we aren't even half as big as one of Gotham's five boroughs. That makes Harm City the per-capita rat and smack capital of the United States of America.

Lord of the Butterflies

© 2014 James LaFond

The recent news from the U.S. Mexican border and the Middle East has driven four poor souls this very week, to ask this crackpot writer what he thinks of the prospects of the U.S. winning its war against the Islamists. Rather than confuse these folks with statements such as, "The U.S. plans and acts in 4 years cycles and the Islamist have a multigenerational mindset. How about if we just take a survey of America's preparations in terms of raising young global warriors. The following survey is had from a third party, the Russian sponsored news site RT.com.

You decide what culture is best prepared to field the warriors of tomorrow...

Indoctrinating the Next Generation of Capitalist Crusaders

-High school student suspended after defending special needs classmate from bullies

Breeder's Digest

Published time: February 13, 2014 19:54

-Six-year-old suspended for a kiss

Published time: December 11, 2013 20:07

-Pennsylvania school sued for suspending student over his toy pen

Published time: September 27, 2013 18:17

-Teen girl, assailant suspended after school calls attack 'mutual fight'

Published time: June 04, 2013 23:00

-S. Carolina student arrested after writing about shooting a dinosaur

Published time: August 21, 2014 23:16

-Two boys suspended for pointing pencils like guns

Published time: May 10, 2013 20:16

-Chicago teacher suspended for showing tools to students

Published time: May 03, 2013 21:29

-Censored cupcakes: US school removed toy soldiers from kid's birthday cake over violence fears

Published time: March 09, 2013 13:07

Edited time: March 09, 2013 15:03

-Never fear, I am quite certain that Islamist children are being schooled in transgender sensitivity and empathetic flower arrangement by committee.

My Toddler is a Violent Racist'

© 2013 James LaFond

One of the most highly developed senses-of-humor I know is attached to one of the most highly developed straight right hands I know, in the person of Oliver, one of my fighters. Some of his stories may be found on the Harm City page. As we were packing up after training one night he called me over and said, "Look James, here's a picture of your next stick-fighter." □

There she stood, a picture of innocence, half as tall as the stick she aspired to whack a sibling with. Oliver then continued, "And you'll love this—she's a racist too!" □

His eyes lit up with mirthful pride as he told the story of his daughter, having watched the Disney/Pixar film Pocahontas and then running around the apartment, "The white devils are coming, the white devils are coming!" sounding the alarm for toddlers of color far and wide.

Oliver continued, "She watches a whole movie and all she remembers is the white devils are coming!"□

He seemed to want an answer so, "Well we are notable villains. We'll have to arrange a cameo appearance so I can show up and provide some role-playing opportunities—like a white devil birthday party!"□

Box Prophecies

Tarl Cabot

The Box Prophecies

© 2014 James LaFond

Last week, a reader, who refers to himself as Tarl Cabot, and was recently released from a corrections facility in the Western United States, contacted me with some ideas for the site. He was miffed at being incarcerated for smoking pot and growing a few plants of his own. He had some feedback for me concerning my nonfiction work, which quickly became a tangent.

"If it comes from the mind they don't want it; Oprah won't get behind it. I'm crashing with two Iraqi war vets who are all messed up from killing people to keep the world safe for rich bastards who don't want me to be able to get high. My one roommate killed nine people—he was a sniper, with three purple hearts. Now, that he's back here, and haunted by what he's been through he can't even get medical treatment. So man, I've had it with this sick government and its sick rules. But nobody will listen, not unless I sit in my cardboard box and write my thoughts in my own blood with a plastic fork."

Tarl and I had a pretty involved discussion about the viability of being a blood-writing homeless box prophet. I eventually offered him an outlet here for his well-considered angst, as opposed to writing in his blood with a plastic fork on the wall of his recyclable home, and then have to deal with the logistics of folding the thing up and mailing it to Oprah without ruining the script. The conversation ended on a high note.

A week later [this past Saturday 1/4/14] I received the following text from Tarl Cabot:

"...For an abundance of wisdom brings an abundance of frustration. So whoever increases knowledge increases pain..."

I have had dealings with five Baltimore area bus prophets. Tarl strikes me as much more of a philosopher. But since Tarl is texting his wisdom to me I'm inclined to wonder if he might just be the next W.D. Fard, only by way of Amsterdam rather than Afghanistan.

If Tarl Cabot texts it to me, I will post it on my blog.

The 2nd Secret of the Universe from Tarl Cabot

© 2014 James LaFond

Apparently our prophet Tarl is still living in a cardboard box somewhere. He texted me from what looks like a Nevada area code. However, based on his latest nugget of wisdom he might be up in Colorado of Wyoming, or perhaps in this frostbitten corner of the United Drug-dens of Gomorrah in the Northeast.

The 2nd Secret is...

"...thermostat"

Tarl, I don't know how your disciples feel about this, and of course you get points for scrawling this on the wall of your cardboard house in your own blood with a fast food spork. But, as your oracle, I was hoping for a bit more to chew on. So, acting as your oracle and high priest, I will interpret this secret to mean that 'Global Warming' doctrine is being called into question by our severe winter.

A clarification or at least an 'adaboy' would be nice.

The 3rd Secret of The Universe From Tarl Cabot

© 2014 James LaFond

Well folks, I too have been waiting on the edge of my theological seat for these past two months wondering if Tarl Cabot died in that cardboard box as he wrote his prophecies in his own blood with a fast food spork. Based on the area code of the phone number this fellow lives out west in the Rocky Mountain States, which had got me thinking, that perhaps he had found Nirvana up in Colorado at the pot dispensary.

Then, lo and behold, the other day I received a voice message, no mere text. The voice was deep in a Heston-like way that would have seemed more appropriate on Easter Sunday, so I had no problem imagining this fellow consulting an almighty force. I was disappointed by the length of the message. I noted it and set it aside for a few days, and come back to it now, none the wiser as to its meaning. Perhaps another believer out there can help me.

According to the Box Prophet, otherwise known as Tarl Cabot, the third secret of the universe is:

"You're it."

I trust this message does not mean that I have been named some kind of postmodern messiah. On the other hand, that could get lucrative...

'The Fat Die Young, and Slowly'

Box Prophecy Four: Tarl Cabot on East Coast Obesity

© 2014 James LaFond

The infamous box prophet has forsaken his bloody spork and his year-old watermelon bin, and his text-only Obama phone with no minutes, for a smart phone, and a conversation with James LaFond...

"Oh, there is so much drama out here on the East Coast—everybody is fat, ugly, and dying. I've been out here from Las Vegas for three weeks now, and I have only seen one pretty girl—and she could have used a treadmill."

JL: "Dude, admittedly you are hailing from the piece-of-ass capital of the world. Billionaires fly around the globe to get laid in Las Vegas. Can't you give the corn-fed girls a break?"

"Corn? Corn! Are you fucking kidding me! Good God, all anybody eats out here is bacon. Put bacon and cheese on it and it's a delicacy; bacon, bacon and more bacon—why not just eat mayonnaise with a spoon!"

JL: "Seriously, it's that bad?"

"Look. I'm fifty and these fuckers make me look twenty-eight. I'm chronologically fifty—effectively twenty-eight. In Vegas I'm forty, out here, I'm not even thirty. I have a better BMI than Pittsburg area teenagers! I'm serious, every old friend I look up. It's like, 'Hey did you hear about so-in-so getting their gallbladder out?', 'Did you know so-in-so just had a stroke?', 'You know I'm, dying right; it hurts so bad—because all I do is fucking eat bacon-on-butter fucking sandwiches and I'm a fat goddamned American head of livestock!'"

"Really, die in peace—why do you have to regale me about your clogged arteries?"

JL: "So how are you doing man?"

"Oh, I'm doing okay, caught a few bluegill today—down here by the RCA pond fishing where it's now fucking illegal to fish. But I'm good, real good. But I think two years is all I'll be able to do out here. Really, eyesight is wasted east of the Mississippi. You people might as well be blind. There is nothing worth seeing out here."

"I see this ninety pound creature with no teeth, on the side of the road, and it's screaming at me. I'm like, 'Is this a horror story or is that a whore?'

"My sister is like, 'That's probably a crack whore.'

"Jimmy, it has a face like a catcher's mitt!"

JL: "Hey Tarl, you ought to see the babes in Baltimore. If you took out the petite little black girls you'd be lucky to find a full set of teeth. It's nothing but dope-fiends."

"Really man, where are the Nazis when you need them?"

I guess it must be rough to chase the American dream across the U.S., only to hit the housing bumble like a pinball bouncing off a bumper, and then end up as the drifter in a zombie apocalypse flick...

'This Empty Suit'

The 5th Secret of the Universe from Tarl Cabot

© 2014 James LaFond

"I'm watching this empty suit right now, spouting empty bullshit about the Middle East. I suppose he's supposed to be the president. He acts more like a storage unit for bad ideas. You know I'm suspicious about this Middle Eastern commitment. It is something you might wish to consider as you imagine the duplicitous extent of your bondage.

"A friend of mine recently came back from deployment in Afghanistan—a Marine Corp sniper. He said that he was just providing protection for the poppy crop, that the poppies literarily grew up to the base perimeter. I guess we have to make sure these rich suburban twats can get high on their heroin. That's [keeping the price of opiates down] worth a leg, right; worth losing your mind in your twenties?

"In any case, the entire justification for going to war seems to be dubious left-handed decapitations, that, upon investigation may well turn out to have been videoed before a blue screen.

"You are being brainwashed—willfully and collectively misinformed, and that oddly enough is the best kept secret of Humanity!"

'Respecting Your System'

Box Prophecy #6: Tarl Cabot's Key to Health

© 2014 James LaFond

The following is from yesterday's phone conversation with my favorite radical humanist.

Okay brother, here is the problem: tap water is treated with chlorine, chlorine kills bacteria, and your gut is a 24 foot long bacteria-dependent sewer system, pretty much articulated to you via your nose by your body in the form of farts.

If you insist on drinking tap water you must have a cup of yogurt before you go to sleep. So for however long you sleep that beneficial bacteria will multiple in your gut—until you dump a bottle of chlorinated water down there and wipe them out!

I realize that most people don't like yogurt because it tastes like eating your girl out when she has a yeast infection. In fact most yogurt looks like one form of vaginal discharge or another.

Look, the fact that you're laughing tells me you've done it so you know I'm right!

Mix up your yogurt with vanilla and some fruit, don't wash it down with chlorinated water, and get your old lady a Monistat kit!

Later brother.

Author's Notebook #5

Why You Don't Get Laid: Repossessing Your Manhood in a Woman's World

© 2013 James LaFond

Genesis

This week I was discussing my current fiction project with a young man: a sci-fi tale told from the perspective of a male prostitute. My friend then began discussing his lonely situation. I invoked the wisdom of the male stripper, male escorts, man-whore, call girl, and madam, that I had interviewed for The Violence Project [which became Harm City]more than a decade ago. Those people specialized in comforting the lonely, both men and women, and had provided me with some interesting insights.

I had decided to do a non-fiction book this winter, and thought it would be The Most Evil Presidents. I began to reassess my authorial priorities, and came to the deeply philosophical conclusion that Joey's aching heart is more important than understanding the evil bastard that owns me and rules the world from a pious chair. To hell with our rulers past and present I say—let's get some nerds laid!

Charles promised me he would put this thing on the fast track to PDF as soon as I send it in. Look for it this winter. [It's looking more like spring 2015.]

Dust Cover

Are you alone? Do you ever find yourself wondering why she's with another guy, or even worse, why she'd rather be alone than with you?

Are you attached and still alone: your status as her lover dwarfed by your role as her handyman or provider; or even worse, your amorous attentions only required after she has viewed a Dwayne Johnson movie?

Why You Are Not Getting Laid provides 20 specific verifiable reasons why you do not have a woman; or if you do, why she would rather read porn than be touched by you.

Quote

"If a guy does not talk a woman might as well sleep with her dog. And no woman marries a dog."

-V.J. Waks

Part One: Why

This is not a book about how to have sex, or even how to convince some woman you are packing worthy DNA. Rather, this is a guide for the self-diagnosis of your intimate malfunction. The goal is to help you understand women better—particularly their diversity—by examining the reason or reasons why they—or maybe just that specific woman—have chosen to keep you at arm's length or beyond, in the empty wilderness of feminine rejection.

Contents:

1. Why Am I Writing This Book?

2. Why Do I Have the Answers To Your Tormenting Question?

3. Why Aren't You Getting Laid?

4. Why Jesus, Allah, God, Satan, Odin and Charles Darwin's Ghost Do Not Care That You Are Not Getting Laid!

Why 3
Why Aren't You Getting Laid?

[seed-text]

The short answer is because you didn't make the sex team.

Now, if that is a game you don't care to play congratulations brother. The value of sex to a fulfilling life is vastly overrated; particularly for men. However, if you would like to be on the sex team you have to be drafted. If you're gay, that's no problem. Because the dudes you want to hook up with think just like you. But if you want a woman, in a woman's world—and make no mistake, America is a woman's world—you need to know why one of them has not drafted you; or has cut you from her two-person team; or just keeps you on the sidelines warming the bench, while she dreams about the man she wishes she was with. Would you want to be that guy, the one she dreams about?

Part Two: Because

Contents:

1. Because You Have Been Mind-fucked By A Sick Society Into Desiring Adult Women Who Are Built Like 14-year-old Girls

2. Because You Are Not Dante Justine

3. Because You Are Broke

4. Because You Are Ugly

5. Because You Are A Punk

6. Because You Are Weak

7. Because You Are A Nerd

8. Because You Are Stupid

9. Because You Are Not Dope Dick Jones

10. Because You Did Not Steal Her Soul

11. Because You Are Not Having Sex With Other Women

12. Because You Don't Have Your Own Place

13. Because You Let Her Move In You Idiot

14. Because You Married Her You Fool

15. Because You Are Not Married To Another Woman

16. Because You Do Not Make Her Laugh

17. Because You Are Too Much Like Her

18. Because You Can't Read Her Mind

19. Because She Gazes Into A Cruel Mirror

20. Because Your Balls Lay Smoldering On Another Man's Altar

You Think Your Job Sucks?

Nightmare Building A Dream a Short Video on Working Conditions in Qatar

© 2013 James LaFond

RT TV ran a documentary segment at 1:20 p.m. on 10/16/13 about the working conditions in Qatar [one of our scumbag slave-owning Islamic allies] for the migrant workers hired to build the 2020 World Cup Stadium. Soccer might be a non-contact sport, but the poor saps that have to build this stadium have it about as rough as a Baltimore crack-dealer.

The report began as a story about two German journalists who were arrested and held by Qatari authorities for the crime of journalism. The interesting part for me was what the German reporter who was telling his story to the British news anchor working for a Moscow news agency had to say about the plight of migrant workers in Qatar:

1. Migrant workers have no rights as we would understand them. They are regarded as dependents [basically a family pet] of a sponsor [usually the

employer] who owns their passport and I.D. and controls access to health care and the legal system.

2. Workers are owed up to seven months of back pay and often never receive promised bonuses. Since they are not permitted to access the legal system except through their sponsor, who is usually the employer as well, they have no recourse.

3. Unpaid workers who quit, or hold out for wages, have their identifications and passports withheld so that they may not legally abide in or leave, Qatar, thereby making breathing a crime. Talk about some leeway for the police.

4. Workers are not provided with clean drinking water at the 110 degree worksites.

5. One worker dies per day on this construction project, primarily from heart attacks. It is estimated that it will cost 4,000 lives to build the 2020 World Cup Stadium.

I once worked with an oil rig man who spent twenty years on various Middle Eastern jobsites. He told me that he would rather work in the U.S. for one quarter the money. What were the worst aspects of working in Islamic nations according to this Vietnam combat veteran?

1. Customs officials and cops always confiscated any magazine that had at least one scantily clad woman in it [even if just a car model in a bathing suit]. "So even if you were just reading Soldier of Fortune, some fucking towel-head pig would scoop it up because the babes and guns catalog advertisement had a woman in shorts."

2. Available hookers were rare, overworked, ugly, and more likely than not to be male.

3. Alcohol was forbidden and greedily confiscated.

4. Living spaces were shared with Arabic workers who wiped their ass with their bare left hand and rinsed the hand off in the same sink where my friend brushed his teeth and filled his canteen, even holding a shit-pasted hand under the running water while the American was brushing his teeth.

Of course, on American TV, Qatar and other such shitholes are depicted as exotic paradises. I suppose so if you are a corporate American reporter who never leaves the hotel.

www.ingramcontent.com/pod-product-compliance
Lightning Source LLC
Chambersburg PA
CBHW060636290526
45793CB00001B/267